MW00918054

# Through the Eyes of
# AMOS ALLEN

AMOS ALLEN

ISBN 978-1-64349-868-3 (paperback)
ISBN 978-1-64349-869-0 (digital)

Copyright © 2018 by Amos Allen

All rights reserved. No part of this publication may be reproduced, distributed, or transmitted in any form or by any means, including photocopying, recording, or other electronic or mechanical methods without the prior written permission of the publisher. For permission requests, solicit the publisher via the address below.

Christian Faith Publishing, Inc.
832 Park Avenue
Meadville, PA 16335
www.christianfaithpublishing.com

Unless otherwise indicated, Scripture quotations are taken from The King James Bible; by permission, 1977 by Consolidated Book Publishers, all rights reserved under the International an Pan-American Copyright conventions. The New King James Bible; by permissions, 1982 by Thomas Nelson, Inc. and the New International Bible; by permission, 1973, 1978, 1984 by International Bible Society – Zondervan.

This book is not authorized to give you any legal advice or is intended to prevent, treat, or cure any medical problems. This is for motivational purposes. This book is suggested the reader consult with an doctor or attorney dealing with medical and legal problems.

Printed in the United States of America

To my mom, Rosa Lee Allen; my wife,
Heather Allen; and my daughter, Alexis Allen

# POTTER

I would like to thank my Lord and Savior, Jesus Christ, who taught me how to be a better man, better human being. He forgave me from all my sins. Thank you, Lord, for guiding me out of my troubled past and teaching me to help others, reminding me to be humble and obedient. Lord, you are always first in what I say or whatever I do. Without you, there is no me. Thank you, Lord, for not giving up on me and abandoning me. This family foundation would not function without your blessing. When I'm feeding people or helping someone in need, I always tell them you sent me in your name, and all the glory and praise is in your name.

# ACKNOWLEDGMENTS

My mom was a strong woman for believing in me when I didn't believe in myself, teaching me that I could do anything I wanted to be; I just had to believe. Thank you, Mom, for making me leave home so I could live and not die in my small world. Thank you for your hard work raising six girls and one boy and showing us tough love when you had to and rewarding us always. Mom, you always said grandma would say I was special. I found out that I am special, and you would be very proud of me. I have Jesus in my life like you always said. Thanks, Mom, I love you.

My wife, Heather Allen, I've never met a person with such a giving and caring heart. God knows I really needed you. You lift me up when I am down, you encourage me to be better, you show me not to be afraid to love and be kind to others. You inspire me to be a better person. Thanks for loving god first and keeping him in our life. Thanks for always being there and really being there, for as my biggest supporter when I was diagnosed with cancer. I know it hasn't been easy taking care of me with what I am going through, driving me around everywhere and not complaining one bit. Every day I whisper to God after ever prayer, and I thank him for allowing me to have someone great like you. Now I finally understand when someone says, "Where is your better half?" Keep being yourself and stay close to God. I love you.

My daughter, Alexis Allen, she really is an awesome young lady. Great attitude, very caring and giving person. She has always been there for me, going through all my sickness and health problems. She never forgot to say "I love you, Dad" every day. She was always asking me, "Do you need anything? Can I do anything?" She will call me when she is out asking me, "Dad, can I bring you anything home?" She is always caring. I took her with me one day to feed the homeless, and one of the guys was telling me he had a job interview on Monday, and he had to walk three miles to the job site. He held up his leg so we could see his shoes. They had big holes in the bottom. Alexis asked me, "Dad, can I?" and I said yes. She took off her new shoes she had just bought and gave them to him. Alexis, God has a lot in store for you. Keep following your heart. Thank you, God, for my daughter. I love you.

*Children, obey your parents, this is the right thing to do because God has placed them in authority over you. Honor your father and mother. This is the first of God's ten commandments that end with a promise. And this, promise: that if you honor your father and mother, yours will be a long life, full of blessing. And now a word to your parents. Don't keep scolding and nagging our children, making them angry and resentful. Rather bring them up with the loving discipline the lord himself approves, with suggestions and godly advice.*
*—Ephesians 6:1–4*

# SPECIAL THANKS

I would like to say thank you to those who have helped me on my journey through life. Without you, it would have been a curse instead of a blessing. Thanks again to you:

Moffitt Cancer Center
William W. Tison III
Marc Wilder
Armondo Roche
Mr. and Mrs. John Heintz
James L Ferguson, VA Hospital

# CONTENTS

# CHAPTER 1

## Growing Up

I remember being six years old, and my grandmother used to always talk to us about the old days. She would give us candy canes and tell us about the things that happened to her and all the things they went through and how much harmony they had in the midst of all the segregation and unjust things going on in the world. She used to always smile and talk about her God and the good things he had done for her and our family. I didn't remember when she passed away, but I always remember she would look at me and say, "You are special, and God is going to use you." I used to be afraid when she said that; I didn't know what she meant by that. I just tried to be a good kid, and as I got older around nine, I started to work selling newspapers, shining shoes, hauling groceries from the grocery stores. I would do anything to make money to bring home to help my mom. She would send us to the movies on Sundays, and when we got back from the movies, the house would be in a wreck. Her boyfriend would fight her while we were gone every Sunday. It got to the point that I didn't want to go anymore. I used to say if I was special, then I could make this go away. Every penny I made, I gave it to my mom. It was something inside of me that was guiding me. When I would see my mother sleep, I would go over and lay my head on her chest to hear her heartbeat. I made a promise to her that I would always take care of her so no one could ever hit her again. She would always talk about God and how he was going to use me. Everyone had this vision but me.

As I got older, I was known for being a good fighter and baseball player. I would always keep a job and give my mom my check. I would take out about thirty to forty dollars to gamble with. I was a good dice shooter. I could make a pair of dice come to attention. I would always win a lot of money, and that helped me be one of the best dressed guys in school and in my neighborhood. I was not afraid to go anywhere and gamble. All through my teens, this was how I took care of myself—gambling—and my work paychecks went to my mom.

I used to always say, someone is with me. I just felt something was or someone was guiding me. I had a guy whom I went to school with who invited me to come over to his place and play him in dice. I remember that same voice telling me not to go, but I didn't listen and went anyway. I got to his house, and we started playing dice; and in about two hours, I had won everything. He said, "Let me call my brother and get some more money." I said, "No problem." I had won everything again, all his money and everything in his apartment. About fifteen minutes later, a knock came at the door, and he went to answer it. When he walked back in, that voice was back, telling me to be strong and stay alert. He had another couple of hundred dollars, and I won that.

As I was picking up the money and not watching him, he shot me twice in the arm and once in the back of the head. I was bleeding very bad. I did not know I was hit in the head, so he said, "Let's go," and I said, "Where are we going?" He said, "I am going to kill you, and then I will kill myself." I looked in his eyes and I could tell he was scared to death. We walked out of the apartment and walked over to my car. I knew I had to get away. I told him I couldn't drive. He said, "Okay, I will drive." I threw the keys up high, so he had to look up; and when he did, I took off, ran to my girlfriend's house, and passed out in the doorway. When I woke up, I was at the Cincinnati General Hospital. My mom and family were there. That's when I was told I was shot in the back of my head. I looked at my mom, and I could see the fear all over her face. That's when I began to get scared.

I had been through a lot. I remember after I had gotten out of the hospital, my mom and I talked. She asked me what I was going to do with my life, and I told her I was thinking about going back into the military. I went in for two years when I was nineteen and stayed until I was twenty-one. I had signed up for Vietnam, but I was sent to Germany. My mom was happy when I told her about what I was thinking. She just wanted me gone from Cincinnati. She said God was holding on to me because he was going to use me. I started thinking about it more and more. I kept working and shooting dice for a couple of years, and one day, I just said, "I'm leaving." I called an army recruiter and asked him what I needed to do. He asked me if I had been in any trouble while I was out, like having been arrested or if I had any court dates? I told him *no*! He said, "I will do a record check and get back to you." He called me back in about a week later and said I was all cleared; and after I signed the papers, he could have me gone whenever I was ready. I met with him, signed the papers, and chose to leave in two weeks. I sat down with some friends, and we all talked about life. I remember saying the first time I went in, I wanted to go to war (Vietnam). I had so much anger, hatred, and competitiveness about me.

Now all I wanted was to get away because I wanted peace and to be settled and help others. I was changing right before my eyes, and all the people who knew what a monster I was saw me changing. We all laughed. Later I could see people didn't want me to leave because they didn't want me to change. But it was something more powerful that was driving me away. It was that same feeling I had when I was lying in the hospital bed after I got shot. Everyone asked me, "When you are going to get him?" And I said, "I'm not." I was at peace with it, and I would let the courts settle it. Something came over me and cleansed me and changed me.

I always flashbacked to what my grandmother used to say about me being special and that God was going to use me. And my mom started the same thing. I thought they were just saying it just to build me up or just speaking over me. I didn't know for sure. All I know was that I was leaving in two weeks, and everything that could happen began to. All sorts of things were going on around me. A lot of my friends were going to jail; three others had gotten killed. It was beginning to get crazy. I remember the first time I prayed to the God my grandmother and mother used to talk about so highly. I prayed in secret because where I grew up, you had to be a tough guy. If you cried, you were a chump or sissy. You believed in no one but yourself.

After I prayed, I felt so relieved. It was like someone was listening to me and guiding me. I didn't know what it was. I started having flashbacks about things that had happened in my life. Like at school one day, I listened to a girl from our neighborhood talking about how they couldn't wear pants to school (they had to wear a skirt or dress) and how they had to wear the same clothes a lot. I had two younger sisters. I knew she was right about what she was saying. Two weeks later, I planned a boycott at our school, Campbell Junior High. I told my crew to put the word out for no one to eat lunch that day. I sent my crew to the neighborhood stores and told them to bring enough bread, meats, chips, snacks to feed the whole school. The police, newspaper, news stations, and all other media outlets were there. Everyone was there. I was sent to see the principal (Mr. Pittman), and everyone was afraid of him. He got his hard-nosed reputation from Aiken Senior High School. I was not afraid of him. I was fighting for a cause.

I arrived at his office, and everyone was there (police, news journalist, a justice representative); they were going to take me to jail. The principal asked me who organized this and what group or social group or adult helped with this. I told him it was all my idea, and he asked me why. I told him that the girls could not wear pants to school, and lot of them could not afford a dress or skirt to wear every day. Because of this, a lot of kids were missing school and ashamed of wearing the same clothes every day. He looked at me and said, "You organized this for them?" I said, "Yes, sir." They didn't press charges on me. The school lost a lot of money for that day for lunch, but I had to get on the PA system and tell everyone to go back to eating lunch, and the next day, the boycott was over. The principal told me he would talk to the board of education, and he would get back with me. It was on the news, in the newspapers, and everywhere. We had enough food to feed an army. Three weeks later, the principal called me into his office and said the board made a change to the school policy, and they were going to let the girls wear pants. He asked me again, "Did you organize that boycott alone?" And I said, "Yes, sir, I did." And he said, "There is something about you. You are a natural leader. Keep leading in the right direction." Something was leading me inside my gut.

I wanted to go to Vietnam; I signed up for it. I wanted to fight. That's what I was comfortable doing. I was not afraid of anything. I knew something was protecting me. Too many things happened to me, and I always came out okay. Every time I used to always hear that voice, telling me go ahead or stop, leave, go home, or come in. It was strange. I used to be with my crew, and something was about to go down bad. Something or someone would pull me away. I remember a friend of mine came over to our housing projects. We hung out awhile, and he asked me to come back over to his neighborhood. It was the same day that I was going to Emmanuel Boxing Center. About six of us. Aaron and I did spar, and it was great. I held my own, and the guys from my hood and I were so happy. It was a big thing back then. Aaron Pryor was one of the best young fighters out of Cincinnati, Ohio. Later, Aaron Pryor went on to be the undefeated world champion and made millions of dollars.

I left the gym and went home. It was snowing, so it took a while to get home. I finally got in the house and went to sleep. The next day, my mom said, "Your friend was on the news," and she began telling me what happened. I went upstairs and turned on the TV to hear the news. There it was with his picture being charged with robbery. I couldn't believe first degree murder. We were just together five hours earlier. That was another time that voice told me to go to the gym and work out. Something was guiding me away from a lot of things. That's when the light came on. It was God, and he has chosen me to follow him. I just realized it was something special, and no matter what, I was leaving. The force was bigger than me.

Two weeks had gone by, and my recruiter was at my door, saying it was time to go. That day creeped up on me, and it was time to leave. I look at my family and Cincinnati, and my gut was telling me it would be a long time before I would be back. I was prepared to leave again. I was taught by some of the tough fighters in the city and had more heart than Campbell had beans. It was time for a change. I have not lived in Cincinnati in forty years.

It's amazing how God will teach you on your journey and show you how it's not about you. It's about the glory and the kingdom of his gospel because he will use you to get to someone else or reverse. We are just students of his amazing glory.

*But you are chosen, a royal priesthood, a holy nation, God's special possession that you may declare the praises of him who called you out of darkness into his wonderful light.*
*—1 Peter 2:8*

# WHOSE EYES ARE YOU SEEING THROUGH

# CHAPTER 2

## *Military*

I was sent back to Germany where I started boxing again and took over the team in Frankfurt. I was the captain of the Frankfurt boxing team, and we had some very good fighters there. I remember we went to Hanoi for a Valentines 14 boxing tournament. We had weigh-ins at 7:00 a.m. that morning to see who you were going to fight that night. I was matched up with a guy named Calvin Chisolm. Everywhere we went that day, I ran into him, and all I heard was his mouth about how he was going to knock me out. But little did he know, I was not afraid; but all day, that was all I heard. Finally, it started getting close to check-in time. Everyone was watching the fights, and it was a packed house. And yes, Calvin was still talking. Even two fights before us, he was still talking. My trainer Sam was one of the best fighters and trainers in Frankfurt. He got out of the army and stayed there. He used to fight and got paid with the German boxing clubs. It was time for my fight, and they announced us out of the corner. The bell rang, and I went straight to him and knocked Calvin Chisolm out in twenty-four seconds in the first round. The whole place went crazy. My team started picking me up. Even Sam my trainer was smiling, and you never saw that happen. But I took something from my home with me—my heart. I was always told when a person talks a lot, it was usually because they were trying to get out of something or trying to make you believe in something. I wasn't buying it. After we got back, I started teaching others in the army how to box.

It was cool we had a chance to work out with Angelo Dundee, heavyweight from Germany. Big German guy, Angelo was Ali's head guy for many years. It was nice having him use our ring and watching us show out. I lost interest again in boxing and started training back in the arts. I lived in downtown Korea while I was stationed there. The army allowed me to live off base, so I lived in town with the Koreans and trained four hours a day and seven hours on weekends. I was one of few African Americans teaching martial arts in Korea. But that was how hard I worked and how I had to be good. And believe me, I had to do everything better than the next person. Mr. Yee used to tell me, "Rick, you must be the best in Korea." It was prejudice and me working at that time for my fourth degree. I had to work out better than everyone that was testing. They did not want me bringing the arts back to the United States, so high-rank Koreans came up with the concept of punching and kicking and using elbows at the same time. It was unheard of until Bruce Lee showed it. And they knew they were going to make millions and millions of dollars on it, and they did.

I learned that technique fast because I was already a good boxer, and I had good hand and feet coordination. We worked out about thirty-five and forty hours a week. All I did was train and train and train. I wanted to be one of the best, if not the best. Living downtown was something you couldn't be afraid of because the base was about one to two miles away. At that time, I was not worried about anything. I had started praying and talking to God. I knew something was going on, and I had protection over me. I could just feel it.

I remember leaving base one night, and I was alone walking home to the Ville. I met up with a guy named Jerome, and we started walking together. Jerome was known by the Koreans for being a big gambler and a good fighter. Walking home, we took a shortcut through an alley. When we crossed over to the next one, we had a gang following us. They were known as the slickey boys. There was about ten of them. Jerome said, "Don't look back and keep walking, and when they get to us, we will put our backs against the wall so they cannot get behind us." Jerome looked at me, and I could tell he was confident I was the one with him. So about three minutes later, they caught up to us; and when they saw us, they said something to Jerome and took off running. At the time, I didn't understand or speak Korean that good, but Jerome did. He lived in the Ville for about five years, and everyone knew him. I never questioned or asked him about his business. All I know was when I walked into a club with him, all the owners gave me free stuff. I could walk around the Ville with no problem after that.

It was something watching over me. I didn't hang out with anyone when I finished my job every day on base. I just went home and changed clothes and worked out for about four to five hours every day. My time was getting short, and I had about twenty days before it was time to leave Korea, and I was too happy to go back to United States. I was bringing back a new form of fighting and self-defense. Someone there did not want me to get back home with this, and they really had it planned out well. But again, it was something protecting me.

When I got up that morning to get ready to leave my room, there was another small bag next to my bag. I didn't recognize it, so I left it there. I got to the airport. I felt strange. My gut was telling me something was wrong. I looked inside my small bag, and it had headphones and other wires in it. When we got to the airport, I left the small bag in the car. There was a young lady with me whom I thought was my friend. But my gut was telling me again whatever is going on, she was a part of it; and when she left, I checked my bags again before I turned them in. When we got on the plane and took off, I could tell something else was going on. I was watching the airline attendants and others whisper. It was like I was an outcast on that plane; people were watching me. The flight attendants would not serve me a drink or either talk to me. I heard one of the flight attendants say, "I'm not ready to die." The plane landed halfway for gas and maintenance. I think my bags were checked. I saw a friend of mine; he was a military police officer. We got there together and hung out a couple of times. While we were together, I asked him what was going on, and he said someone called in before we left and said I had a bomb on the plane. I looked at him and said, "Man, are you serious?" He looked at me and started smiling and said, "Yes, but I know you and was telling people on the plane that it wasn't true." We finally got back on the plane and headed back home. I prayed all the way back home.

It felt like five hundred pounds was lifted off my back. They had that plan worked, but God had another plan in store for me. That's when I started really believing and seeing the grace of God. But just like a lot people, I straddled the line instead of giving my all. I had to learn more and go through more.

Teaching had gotten easy for me because I understand the concept of the technique, and I developed new combinations. I taught in New Jersey for about two years, and I was the bouncer and night manager at the NCO club at night. My name got around fast because of my teaching skills, and I didn't play games. When I walked into a room, you knew it. I had a strong presence and carried myself well. But there was something guiding me and leading me. My manner was reassured, and my values were changing right before my own eyes. I started getting more disciplined and taking things more seriously. I was the one who gave physical fitness to my unit every morning and taught in the evenings and worked the clubs at night. I found myself talking more to God about my family life and everything that came to mind. I remember in the projects they used to ask me where I got my heart from, and I couldn't answer. I just had it. But being the only boy with six sisters, I had a lot of fights taking up for them. When things got dark and I didn't understand it, I always asked God. I heard my mom always say, "I'm waiting on God. He would answer, provide, or open a door. That was stuck in my heart and mind."

Leaving New Jersey, my next stop was Augsburg, Germany. New place, but I had the same concept of teaching this new art. When I asked around about the programs, everyone came back to this German police Herman. He had everything locked down when it came to self-defense. He was the man. I got a chance to meet with him on base where he also taught, and we talked for about two hours. He drilled me with a lot of questions and wanted to see me teach. He invited me to teach one of his military classes in the evening. I showed up and impressed not only him but everyone who was there. The next day, he asked me if I would like to take his military classes over, and I said yes. I hired an assistant instructor and taught him the new art. He was a brown belt in another art, and I was a fourth dan in pro Tae Kwon Do. My assistant was my right-hand man, and we started taking over Augsburg, Germany, in teaching and bodyguard work. We took over one of the biggest clubs there called the Cthree. I remember my first time going there. I watched some military guys tear the place up. The security was a joke. It was glass everywhere. They had to shut it down. I told one of the waiters to set up a meeting with the owners. He did not want that because he was part of the security. I waited a couple of days, and I went back to see the owner. We sat down and talked. I told him if he hired me, what happened a couple of nights ago would never happen again. Warner, the owner, and I agreed on a deal. I bought a friend of mine in with me, and we hired all new DJ Security, and the word got around base that we were running the Cthree club, and so all the fights and trouble had to come through us first. That stopped a lot of things happening. The military guys there knew about me and my assistant teachings and had a lot of respect for us. The next thing happened: we started doing all the bodyguard work for most of the celebrities coming to town. Big names I worked for, but my heart was changing. I started to just want to teach. I finally left Augsburg, Germany.

*As the Father love me, so have I, loved you. Now remain in my love. If you obey my commands. You will remain in my love just as I have obeyed my Father's commands and remain in his love. I have told you this so that my joy may be in you and that your job may be complete. My command is this, love each other as I have loved you. Greater love has one than this, that he lay down his life for his friend.*

—John 15:3–9

# WHOSE EYES ARE YOU SEEING THROUGH

# CHAPTER 3

# *Tampa*

My next destination was Tampa, Florida. I was here all alone: no family, no friends, no military. Just me and the Lord. I just wanted to teach. My first job was working for the Juvenile Justice Center, W. T. Edwards. That was where they sent kids who weren't old enough for the county jail. I mean, some kids were there with serious charges: drug dealers, carjackers, armed robberies, and on and on. So many of these kids were street smart. The older ones wanted to go to the county jail where they could smoke and have more freedom. They didn't care about getting another charge, like hitting a staff member or throwing some type of feces on you. I knew some of the staff were afraid of being there. They turned into the candy man. They would give the kids extra candy or food to do what they say. It's funny because these kids were smart. Out of one hundred boys who were there, you might have ten fathers in the home. On visiting day, all you would see were mothers and grandmothers.

I remember talking to God one night about this job. I had just seen one of the other guys who had been there for a long time get punched in the face. I was in the office looking out the glass. I had to rush inside to calm things down before it got worse. I pushed the alarm, and we made everyone lie facedown on the floor. We had to lock down the dorm. Especially the "big boys," the worst dorm you could be assigned to. Not everyone could work in there. My Holy Spirit was telling me this was where I was going to be working. I knew I had to come up with a game plan, or it would be over. You could not even hit one of these kids back, or you would be going to the county jail.

I remembered on a three to eleven shift, I was assigned to the B2. I asked the dorm supervisor if I could put the kids in a circle and show them a demo of what I used to teach in Germany and all around the United States and just talk to them. He smiled and said, "Please do!" We had already talked about my background. I had the kids make a circle. They didn't know me that well. I was an unfamiliar staff member with no respect, so it was difficult working there in the beginning. I kept saying to myself, if I could get them quiet for five minutes and get their attention, this would work. I hollered real loud, and when it got quiet, I started my shadow boxing, and then I went into my martial arts. I had their complete attention. That demo was great. There were some staff in the hall watching, and when I finished, all the kids were yelling and clapping their hands.

After I finished, I started talking to them, telling them I came from a broken home like a lot of them, and it was up to me. I had to choose not to be a victim. I told them about Korea and Germany, how I learned how to speak both languages. I told them how I talk to God. I knew a lot of them came from homes where their mothers or grandmothers told them about God just like I learned. I told them it's not where you come from; it's where you're going. That night, I looked around the circle, and I had seen tears running down some faces, and you couldn't hear a pin drop. The next day, when I got to work, my supervisor called me in before my shift started. I knew I was in trouble from last night. I got in her office, and she said, "Mr. Allen, I heard about your show you put on last night and your talk with the boys. A lot of staff that didn't know you were very impressed with the way you carried yourself and your love for those kids. The kids had been asking when you were coming in. They really respect you." And I told her, "I used to be one of them." I earned a new name after that night. The kids started calling me "Great Fighter." Even the staff started calling me that. Every day I worked, all they wanted was to hear stories about Germany and all the places I had been. I was beginning to see my calling.

I wanted to open my own school here in Tampa, so I had to come up with rent money, deposit, insurance money, uniforms, new equipment. I had a nice jewelry collection: a Raymond Weil watch, diamond rings, and a lot of other pieces of jewelry. I took it to this one jeweler, and he asked me how much I was trying to get, and I told him what I was trying to do, and he offered me a price and said if I got the money back, he would sell it back to me. When I walked away, I knew that was the last time I would see that jewelry. My spirit was telling me that what I was about to do was more important than that jewelry. I had enough money to start my school in Tampa.

I applied for another job at the courthouse. I heard a retired colonel was in charge of security service. I talked to the colonel and got the job. It was a pay raise and an easy job as security at the courthouse. This was where I met this guy named Marc. He was one of the security officers at the courthouse as well, and I was telling him about pro TKD, and he told me he was a first degree in the Tae Kwon Do. I told him to get with me because I would be looking for an assistant instructor. I knew something special was happening because everything was lining up perfect.

I met with Mr. Howard. He was the owner of Ethan Allen Furniture Stores and owned this space I was looking to rent. I told him about my vision, that I wanted to help troubled kids and low-income families. He thought about it overnight and called me the next day, and we met and exchanged money and signed contracts. Later I talked to Marc and told him I would like for him to join me.

We opened the school, and Marc was in charge of forms and a lot of new techniques I taught him. Our school was known for all its hard work, and we did not sell belts. We made you work for them. It was funny when we would go to a tournament, people would come over where we sat, thinking that's where they were supposed to pick up their trophies. That's how many we had, wherever we would go. Marc and I used to sit back and turn our students loose. Even at home, we would set up sparring sessions with other schools and leave out of those schools with twenty wins and one loss. That one loss was probably in weapons or something. But in fighting, we were the school to beat. Every other school was teaching forms, weapons, and other Western-style stuff. But we taught how to defend yourself. How to fight. I was a master of fighting. I've done it all my life. Other schools made a lot of money to look pretty, and they were selling belts. We didn't make a lot of money; most of our students couldn't afford to pay. I worked with a lot of the parents and programs, reducing fees and payments. Marc had such a love for teaching and helping kids; I was only able give him one hundred dollars a month. But we made it work, and we touched a lot of lives. These kids were depending on us. I remember when I first went into the school. I prayed out very loud and said, "God, you want me here, and I am here. Bless this place and guide me through this and help me touch lives and families." And he did. A lot of the kids loved the school, Marc, and me because we gave it to them straight, teaching them that success started right here. The harder they worked, the more they would get out of it. I used to tell them about God and praying and how they were never alone. How God always watches over them. I told them not to be afraid to talk to God or ask him for things.

At our school, there was a lot of broken families or single-parent homes. We had the children's home, ACTS programs, or juvenile programs. I had one of the supervisors from one of the programs tell me how they were afraid to have their kids come here and learn martial arts. But since they had been in our program, he hadn't had one fight out of the kids. I told him we didn't teach only how to fight, but we taught when to fight and that the bigger person walks away. If you know you could destroy someone with what you know, why do it? And if we heard you were in a fight, you better have had a good reason, and all our students knew that. This is the reason why we won a lot of tournaments. Our students knew when to fight. We had over one thousand trophies combined. We even had three students to win the US Open World Championship, where people come from all over the world to compete.

So many parents came to tell us how their kids were doing better at home and in school. Their homework was getting done, and their grades were better. We checked all students' reports cards, and if you had a low grade in any subjects, you had to study that subject during your martial art class while everyone else had fun and learned new techniques. We put a stop to bad grades. All the glory to God; he was teaching them. Most of the students are now very successful and have their own families. Some tell of these childhood stories to their own children and families today. This is one of the teachings God taught me about being obedient and humble.

*Be self-controlled and alert. Your enemy the devil prowls around like a roaring lion looking for someone to devour.*
—1 Peter 5:8

*However, I consider my life worth nothing to me. If only I may finish the race and complete the task the Lord Jesus has given me. The task of testifying the gospel of God's grace.*
—Acts 20:24

# WHOSE EYES ARE YOU SEEING THROUGH

# CHAPTER 4

## *Jobs*

Something was driving me to leave the courthouse job. A gut feeling. I took a leave of absence and sat at home for about three weeks. I asked God everyday what I was to do next and where I was going. The thought of being a bail bondsman kept running in my head. I did some research on the pros and cons of the business, and it didn't look good. One bad bond would put you out of business. It was a very risky business to be in. But I kept wanting to do it. Now even my heart was driving me to do this. I prayed about and told my wife how I felt about it. We talked awhile about the dangers and everything that came with the job. She said, "That's you! That job would be great for you." That was the kind of life I knew. I prayed about it again and asked God would he be our partner and let me use this job for my ministry. I was thinking this would be a good job to spread Jesus's name. Then I sat back and thought, *That is why this job is on my mind so much*. It was all coming together.

I had to find someone to let me intern at their bail bonds office and was difficult because they had to pay you minimum wage while you intern with them. But it had some advantages with it also. They could use you to do all the office paperwork or use to do some bounty work picking up bail jumpers. And there were also disadvantages. When you finished your internship, you could leave and open your own bail office. That would be competition for them.

A lot of bail bond companies would not bring you in. They also knew you didn't have the money that was required by an insurance company to start you off. I remember I met this judge at the courthouse, and one day we were talking. He told me, "If I could ever do anything for you, let me know," and I said thanks and left it at that. I didn't think I would ever need a favor from a judge or anyone in the courthouse. But I went down to the courthouse one day, and I ran into him. He said, "I haven't seen you in a while. Is everything okay?" I told him I had been going through some back problems, and I had back surgery. I told him I did not think I was coming back to work there. My heart was pulling me toward the bail bonds industry. I have heard it was hard getting into. He said, "I know someone who could probably help you," and that was music to my ears. I gave him one of my martial arts cards that had all my information on it. I told him thanks and left.

In about a week, I got a call from a big-time insurance company. The vice president of the company said, "I heard you were trying to intern somewhere," and I immediately said, "Yes, sir." We set up an appointment for the next day to talk. We talked about the bail industry, and while sitting there, I found out that I was talking to the owner of the insurance company. He had about one hundred bail bonds companies that was under his insurance company. He was a very intelligent man, with a strong voice, and he looked you straight in the eye while talking to you. I knew this was a divine setup for me to be sitting here talking to the owner of the company. He started out being a bail bonds-man and turned it into a twenty-five-million-dollar business.

He kept his bail bonds office and let his family run it. He made a call to the next building over and told the head person to come over and meet me. After all that happened, he asked me when I wanted to start. We set it up to start the following Monday. That office is where I learned all the ropes of the bail bonds industry. This place was at the top of the game. I was with two females in the office. They knew everything about the industry. They taught me all the tricks clients would pull on you, what was a good bond and what was a risky bond. I went out for bounty work with one of their husbands. He was a bondsman as well and ran his own office under the same insur-ance company. When I went out with him, he would split the pickup fee with me, and that was great. If a person's bond was ten thousand dollars, they would have to pay the bondsman one thousand dollars or 10 percent of the bond. I had gotten so good at it. I always went out with him to pick up bail jumpers. That was an extra five or six hundred dollars a week sometime.

Well, my internship was coming to an end. I set up another meeting with the owner to talk about the future. He asked me if I wanted to work for him, and he would let me be a supervisor. I told him I would think about it and get back to him. After I took the state test and passed it, something was coaching me inside to open my own office. But I know I didn't have a B.U.F. account means when a person skips on a bond and you couldn't find them in time, you are required to pay for that bond to the insurance company. No insurance company would let you work for them without setting up account. By that time, I was pretty good at bounty hunting, and everyone knew that. When I talked to the owner of the insurance company and told him I wanted to work for myself, he told the vice president to give me whatever I needed to start. That's when Amos Bail Bonds started. I rented a place until I was able to buy a building. My wife, Heather, took care of the office, and I did the labor. I prayed and asked God again if he would be a partner in this business with us, and I would use it for my ministry. Well, the word got out in the jail that if you were not planning on showing up for court, do not call Amos Bail Bonds. My reputation was that I would find you and bring you back to justice no matter where you were.

I had a guy bond out and left the United States. He called me from Jamaica and said, "Mr. Amos, I am sorry I had to leave, but DEA wanted me to turn in my connection, and I couldn't do that, so I had to leave." That bond was going to cost me twenty thousand dollars, and I only had sixty days to return him or pay the money. I had some people I knew from the DEA office, so my wife and I talked to the agent. He said they might have someone there, so we would get a call. Two days later, I got a call, and it was an agent from DEA. He said, "I am sitting in a bar in Jamaica, and guess who I am looking at?" I said, "Who?" He said, "Your guy. I cannot arrest him now because if I do, he would have to go to the Jamaica jail, and he could buy his way out. I will be leaving in a couple days, and I will call you when I get him back." Four days later, I got a call, and they said, "Your Jamaican package is in the county jail." I went to the jail, and there he was. That gave me the opportunity to turn in my paperwork to come off the bond.

The miracle about the whole thing is, when the bond was written, I was in the hospital and had a bleeding in my brain. The doctors were telling my wife it did not look good for me. Everyone was expecting the worst. I remember one night all the lights were shinning on me, and I was talking to the lights and telling them I wanted to see my mother. You see, my mom had passed away in 2000. I kept telling the lights I wanted to see my mom. All I felt were bright lights and feeling real warm, heat all over my body. I did not see a face, just the lights telling me I could not see me mom; I had to go back. It wasn't time yet. I finally woke up. There were a lot of visitors coming in and out of my room. I was introducing them to celebrity that already passed away.

I remember when I got out the hospital, all I could think about was God. My wife said that one day, I was lying on the floor trying to call my mom. She called the doctor and told him what was going on. He told her, my wife, it was okay to tell me my mom had passed away. I lay there and prayed and asked God to help me, mold me, forgive me of my sins, and to make me whole. Everything started to change.

I got back to work and just watched God show out. All the kids that I had at the juvenile center were now old enough for the county jail. The word got around that Great Fighter was a bail bondsman. Our office took off, and our ministry really started to help the community. We gave food baskets to the seniors, single moms, and helped a lot of low-income families as well. I went to the jail a lot to talk to the ones who couldn't get out. I talked to everyone who would listen about God and how he saved my life and changed me, and he could do the same for them. A lot of them listened because I once was just like them.

The local newspaper started doing news articles on me, and our foundation was being birthed.

I used to go to places the police wouldn't go to unless they had two or three cars. I was not afraid because I knew God was with me. I remember going to this one apartment to bring a guy in, and the police came to help me. We wanted to go in, but the officer said he had to wait on some more backup. We told him we were going in, and he said, "You touch that door again, I am leaving." My guy started banging on the door, and the officer left. An older gentleman came out, and I asked him, "Is he in there?" He gave me a that yes look. We kicked the door open, went in, and found him under the bed. We got him out, put handcuffs on him and took him to jail. I wasn't afraid. I knew God was with me. Everything was starting to change. The younger generation was coming to talk to me about life in general and how I changed my life. I told them about Jesus and God and how my life changed, and it was a process like everything else. First, you give God your life and really mean it. You cannot straddle the line, like we all do. We must choose life or death. That's how Jesus saw it, and you had to go through Jesus to get to God. I always say be humble, be obedient, have love in your heart. I would say, how could you be a crack dealer and love people? Because you are giving them poison. Everywhere I went, I would spread the word of the gospel.

One mom came to my office and said, "My son has a lot of respect for you," and how he was changing, not hanging around the same crowd, and even stopped smoking. This was one of the big crack dealers who never had a job before, and I was touching his life. I started talking to them about working an honest job for an honest living. When they got older, they'd have something to fall back on. The word was getting around that I was a pastor who didn't play games. I listened to gospel music a lot, and when someone was in my car whom I was taking back to jail, that was all they would hear until we arrived at the county jail. This was really my ministry, and there was no room for nonsense. I would have parents and wives call me and ask me if I could talk to their loved ones about staying out of trouble and changing their lives. I knew God would open those doors, and I was going to run through them. Amazing how my life was changing.

I walked away from smoking cigarettes, drinking gin and juice, and a lot of other things. My strength for God has grown stronger and stronger. I went from giving nothing to the church to paying my 10 percent. Still while blessing others and believing that the bail bonds work was just part of the journey. Even until this day, I still see the two lives I helped save. The two drug dealers gave up the streets. Both are working and being full-time fathers to their kids and helping in the community with others spreading the gospel.

The bail bonds industry was great. We made a lot of money to help others. I received a lot of calls from my sister, telling me some of my friends' mothers and other family members who passed away. My wife and I made it our business to send money and help those families out. I knew God had me here for more reasons than one. It gave me great glory to be able to help these kids I've seen grow up in the system. Most of them didn't have a father in the house, and most of the men they knew were in prison. This was a normal life for most. Most of the kids didn't have a chance in the low-income areas. It didn't matter what nationality—black, white, tan, or pale. It was put in my spirit that I needed something or someone to believe in and someone that I could believe in. I leaned to God to love me every day the same. In good days, bad days, or whatever, his love for me was always the same. He would always accept me.

*He said to me, "My grace is sufficient for you, for my power is made perfect in weakness." Most gladly therefore I will rather glory in my weaknesses, that power of Christ may rest on me.*

—2 Corinthians 12:9

# WHOSE EYES ARE YOU SEEING THROUGH

# CHAPTER 5

## *Street Ministry*

We had opened a restaurant next door to the bail bonds office called Cincinnati's. That's where I am from: Cincinnati, Ohio. We were planning on bringing in more revenue to help more people and be able to feed them at a cheap price. We also wanted to help put people to work. We had to realize a lot of people didn't want to work. My dream was to create a lot of jobs, but my soul spoke to me that this door was going to close. This was something we were trying to do on our own, and we soon learned we had to include God. That's what I promised, that I would put God in everything I did or said. It was hard not straddling the line. I think how we all live one day and say something and the next do the opposite. I fought with this because I wanted to be better, and I knew it had to start with my thinking and trusting God. He will open some doors and close some, and you cannot force doors open, or you will be alone in everything that happens.

Eight years later, we closed the restaurant down and rented it out. Trying to help first-time business owners out was another experience where God guided me through. He was teaching me how to run multiple companies under one foundation. My goal was to feed and help as many people as we could. And I always prayed. I can do all things through Christ who strengthens me. Giving first-time owners the opportunity to have their own business was something that took a lot of work and strength doing. We met some good and some bad people on this journey. It was mostly bad ones. They did not want to pay their rent, always trying to get but without putting the work in. I would pray for a lot of them. And I would tell them they had to put God in with them, or it wouldn't be successful, but most had their own ideals. I stopped giving advice and let them do their own thing. We just focused on keeping the property looking nice and clean outside. That gave me more time to do what my heart guided me to do.

My first love was helping others, feeding and clothing the homeless, and spreading the gospel. My heart and mind knew it was time to do more street ministry. I prayed about it and started doing just that. I would run from that thought, telling God I didn't want to be a preacher. I found myself more and more preaching to people about different things that were going on with my life. Sometimes people would come to me about things that they were going through. Most of the things I talked about were situations that I had already gone through. It's funny because I learned that God would let me go through things personally, so when I would be talking to someone who had gone through the same problem, I would know what he wanted me to do because I had already experienced it. My whole life had changed right before my own eyes.

I was learning to love and care about others, something that was very hard for me to do. The way I grew up and the way I lived, it was all about me, surviving, and looking out for my family. As I was getting older, I could now see the pattern that God has always had for me. Even when I was running from God, as I look back, I did help others. God showed me my past. I know it sounds strange, but it really happened. He also showed me every time he saved my life: when I got shot in the head; when I was in a bad car accident, when my gas pedal was stuck, and I drove over two cars and knocked over a telephone pole; when I had a bleed in my heard, and the doctors were telling my wife it didn't look good for me; when I couldn't walk after having two back surgeries; the time I was medivac back from overseas in a plane with other soldiers missing limbs, and the infection in my hand that was so bad they might have had to amputate it. There were a lot of things that happened in my life. I flashbacked to one of the older guys in our community who said I was not going to live past twenty-one and how God guided my life and saved me.

I am no longer running from him; I am running to him. I am not where I want to be with him, but I am not definitely where I used to be. I understand no one is perfect, and we must work on our own self every day. Every day is a challenge for everyone. Just remember Isaiah 54:17. Remember, prayer is putting things in the hands of God and letting him do his will. A lot of times, we pray or ask God to do something, but we must remember when we give it to God. Let him have it. He does not need our help. And be patient because God doesn't work on our time. He works on his time. Joseph waited thirteen years,

Abraham waited twenty-five years, Moses waited forty years. If God doesn't answer you right away, stay humble and patient.

The restaurant property is still being rented out with first-time business owners and the same for the one-bedroom house in the back. God taught me patience and to be humble. And when someone shows me they are not serious, we move on to the next tenant or first-time owner and not to get mad. I think everyone is the same, and they are not.

I learned on this journey was be to obedient and not to judge anyone.

It takes a village to raise a kid. Thanks to the Winton Terrace and to the families: Allen family, King family, Brown family, Blassingame family, Johnson family, Worthen family, Jones family, Lewis family, Reese family, Saloman family, Big Dummy, Mccloud family, Tidwel family, and on and on. How over the years we prayed for one another, fed one another, and had respect for one another. As I pray today, Father, give us strength to guide the next generation and to teach them all about you and your glory in Jesus's name.

*Beloved, if our hearts don't condemn us, we have boldness toward God; and whatever we ask, we receive from him, because we keep his commandments and do things that are pleasing in his sight.*
—1 John 3:21–22

# WHOSE EYES ARE YOU SEEING THROUGH

# CHAPTER 6

## Foundation

*Amos Allen Family Foundation.Org*

The Amos Allen Family Foundation—my wife, Heather, and I, our goal was to help feed and clothe the homeless. I had long dreamt this from my younger days. I used to see my mom feed everyone, and she would always say, "These are someone's kids also." That always got stuck in my mind. Whenever I went overseas or here in the USA, I always tried to help someone out. I believe it's something God put in my spirit, looking out for others, even when it was my last. My wife and I decided to make sandwiches once a week and take them to feed the homeless. We would go to the store and pick up lunch meats every week for about twenty-five people. I remember praying and asking God to broaden my coast and to let me feed more people. We were feeding about twenty-five at that time. My prayers were answered the following year, and we were feeding about fifty people.

Our concept changed for the better. We started passing out sack lunches with one sandwich, chips, peanut butter crackers, and a bottle of water. On holidays, we would do special things like personal hygiene bags, with toothbrushes, toothpaste, comb or brush, deodorant, Chapstick, bandages, weekly visits. I would take new T-shirts, underwear, socks, shoes, blankets, sleeping bags. The goal was to try to meet their needs. The best part about it was that God always met the needs of me giving to others. I stayed supplied once a week. I would go by churches and ask for whatever they had extra, any reading material and Bibles. I would take all these things with me and pass them out. I prayed over them and would tell them, "This is not your destination. It's part of your journey. Do not get comfortable because your season will change. Keep asking God to give you the strength to endure what you're going through. Keep God first."

A lot of people asked me my name, and I would just say, "Jesus sent me." They started calling me the man with the black truck. The reason why I don't tell them my name is because Jesus makes all this possible, and that's where all the praises should go, not to me. Now everyone knew the black truck. When they see it, they would run to it. Before, I would pick someone out to lead us in prayer; and after that, we would pass out food and water. In my fifteen years, everyone knew by now, and they started trusting me more. I would go mostly alone during the week and take my family with me on some weekends. It's awesome because when I go to feed, there would be fifty or more, and all the older people would tell the new ones to get in a straight line before I would start giving anything away.

I had police officers and others who liked what I was doing, impressed that I would go under bridges and in the woods or wherever God wanted me to go to find them. I was never afraid. I would tell them about the old me before I gave my life to God, about how many times I got shot, and the only person I was afraid of was God. I would also tell them how you go through Jesus to get to God. I was not going to let anyone stop me from serving Jesus. If you want to play games or do not want to listen, get out of my line. Because the people here wanted to eat and wanted to hear what I had to say. We did not have time for nonsense.

That word got around town. I watched others come and feed. I just shook my head and prayed for them. I watched the people snatching things, running up to the person, and taking their things away from them. Some people never came back. It could be scary for someone with a lot of people running up to you. I was not going to let anything stop me from this mission. My spirit told me this was my ministry. This was what I promised to God I would do if he helped me when I was down and out. Now I had to figure out how to make it better. I knew if I kept praying about it and staying obedient and humble, things would work out.

I was blessed to have a bakery tell me they would give us all their leftovers and orders that were not picked up by other customers. I sometimes would pick up ten to twenty dozen doughnuts and pies a week. Every Christmas Eve, after they would close, they would let us clean the store out, letting us take home about six thousand doughnuts, pies, rolls, and pastries to give out to the homeless. I would bring them home, rebox everything, and on Christmas Day, we would take the stuff with us and pass all of it out to everyone on the streets. The rest I would give to people at the VA hospital and staff who worked at the shelters or other programs. All other things I gave out came from my family. I had been doing this for about fifteen years, feeding and clothing through our foundation. God has brought me a long way from helping kids and people in jail. Every day, I pray and ask God to broaden my horizon and put his hands on me and let me do more.

I remember going out one day, and I took my daughter, Alexis, with me. We were feeding a large group; and a young guy, about eighteen or so, was on a bike. When the line got smaller, he would ask me if I wanted him to find more people. I would tell him yes, and he would ride off and come back with ten or more people. The guy on the bike just kept staring at me, and after everyone left, he said, "Sir, they hurt me." I said, "What!" He said, "They hurt me." Alexis and I were sitting on the tailgate of the truck. I got up and told Alexis to go sit inside the truck because I did not know what he was going to say. I walked up to him and asked what happened, and he said some guys had raped him in the bathroom, and he kept staring at me. He had felt he could trust me, and I was probably the only one he had told. I looked right into his eyes and said, "God hears you, and he will take care of you."

I was in shock. All I wanted to do was get away. It caught me off guard. I thought I could fix anything. I believed I was this super Christian and had all the answers. My eyes were beginning to run; I started crying. I told him to be strong, and I would see him next week. I got into the truck, and Alexis asked, "Daddy, what is wrong." I just said, "That guy is hurt." The whole time I was talking to him, I was looking in his face, but I was seeing my son and my daughter and remembering what my mom used say about these being someone's kids.

The drive home was a quietest ride I had ever been on. My daughter knew it was something very bad; she never saw me that quiet before, especially after feeding and spreading the word. When I got home, I walked straight into my bedroom and lay in bed and just started crying. I was so angry at God for putting me in the situation to hear that. My daughter told my wife something had happened to one of the young guys. She came in the room and asked me what happened. I told her, and she started crying. I was so angry I stayed in my room for two days. I did not want to talk about it or talk about God or anything that had something to do with helping others.

I remember the next morning lying in bed, and I heard a voice say, *Why are you so mad?* over and over. I spoke out, "You let me hear that, and I can't do anything about it." The voice spoke back to me and said, *I know. That's why I did it. While you're out here feeding people and listening to their testimonies, most of the time, they just want someone to listen. I had to teach you how to be a good listener and let you see you can't fix all problems. Only I can do that. While you are on your journey, be a good listener. I gave you two ears and one mouth. Let your heart and ears be your strength.* I got up that morning and felt so relieved and happy because deep down inside, I've been taught a very valuable lesson that I would remember the rest of my life. Jesus taught me, on my journey, to just listen, hear what people have to say. Some will be good, and some might not, but hear them out. Every time I go to feed the homeless, I see the same young man. He just smiles at me and says, "I tell everyone you make the best sandwiches," and we just laugh together. After all that time, when I told him God will fix him and help him, I left torn apart, thinking I let him down. All he wanted was to just have trust in me to listen and not try to fix something I couldn't.

My Holy Spirit was right like always. This valuable tool I needed to stay on my journey. I would go wherever the Lord would send me, and most of time, all I would have is my Social Security and military disability check. After I paid my bills, I would make sure the extra would be used on the foundation missions. At first, my wife was upset with me until her heart gave her the same mission. I remember one Christmas she baked five hams, and we cut them up to make sandwiches. This was one of the happiest days in my life: to see my wife, son, and daughter with me on Christmas Day preparing to go serve others, not worried about ourselves. I was trying to teach the kids the meaning of Christmas and giving to others.

A lot of people say, "Well, when I get rich or get a lot of money, I'm going to do this or that." What they fell to realize is, God wants you now. He wants you to help people with what you have now. Or they say, "When I stop drinking or using drugs, or when I get better clothes, I'm going to start going to church." God doesn't want you to fix up and come to him. He wants you just the way you are. This is what I preach in the streets, under the bridges, or wherever I feed the homeless or anyone. I minister to just everyday people wherever I go. It doesn't matter. I just like spreading the word. The foundation guided me through a lot of stops on my journey.

I remember a Tuesday in the park near the Salvation Army, where I fed a lot. I talked to a lady whom I was feeding that day. She was in her thirties, and she was telling me how she became homeless. She was very smart and educated. She told me she had two degrees from college and what happened in her last job, how she was a hard worker. A new boss came in and gave hear a tough time and fired her. It messed up her head. She started falling behind on things, to the point where she lost everything. She just gave up on everything—her family, her dreams, her life—and became homeless. She had become afraid of life and didn't want responsibility.

She started talking about politics. Florida was holding the Republican convention here in Tampa. She was telling me how the police were stopping them from sleeping where they always stayed and how they were giving them tickets. She told me, "Now we are homeless and don't have anything, and now we have a ticket we cannot pay. They get us off the streets and put us in jail for the accountability to get more money from the state and government." She was a smart young lady and knew the system. After getting laid off from her job, she just gave up on life. I listened to her for a while, and she made some good points and some not so good, and I told her, "We have our trials and tribulations in life, but we must have faith." I asked her who was the poorest person in the world? She said, "The homeless," and I said, "No. The poorest person is a person without dreams." She looked at me and started to smile. I said to her, "Give yourself another chance. It's a big world out there." One day she will be able to tell someone her testimony and help them. I saw a sparkle in her eye. I knew she was going to be okay. I gave her a big hug and prayed over her and left.

*Therefore, I tell you, do not worry about your life, what you will eat or drink; or about your body, what you will wear. Life is more than food, and the body more than clothes? Look at the birds of the air; they do not sow or reap or store away in barns, and yet your Heavenly Father feeds them. Are you not much more valuable than they? Can any one of you by worrying add a single hour to your life? And why do you worry about clothes? See how the flowers of the fields grow. They do not labor or spin. Yet I tell you that not even Solomon in all his splendor was dressed like one of these. If that is how God clothes the grass of the field, which is here today, and tomorrow is thrown into the fire, will he not much more clothe you —you of little faith? So, do not worry saying, what shall we eat? Or what shall we drink? Or what shall we wear? For the pagans run after all these things, and your Heavenly Father knows that you need them. But seek first his kingdom and his righteousness, and all these things will be given to you as well. Therefore, do not worry about tomorrow, for tomorrow will worry itself. Each day has enough trouble of its own.*

—Matthew 6:25–34, NIV

# WHOSE EYES ARE YOU SEEING THROUGH

# CHAPTER 7

## Testimonies

The testimonies I listened to after I fed and prayed over the group of people were enlightening. I really met some good people down on their luck and just gave up. Then you had those who were released from jail or mental hospitals. I would run across teens who left home and ran away, and you could tell they didn't belong there. Some would get eaten up by the streets. I started a segment called "Walking the Streets with Amos." I would interview people to find out how they got where they were. A lot of times, people look at homeless people and think they were born there. I wanted the stay-at-home judges to get a look at homeless people. They could see they were not crazy. I think a lot of people are one paycheck from being homeless. Here are some of the testimonies.

I talked to a man today. He was an older gentleman in front of Publix. He was ringing the bell while people were putting money in the Salvation Army can. He was walking up and down the sidewalk, and I went into the store. When I came out, he was sitting down in a chair, ringing the bell. I put a dollar in the can to start a conversation. I don't know why; I just felt a need to talk to him in that moment. I said, "God is good. He woke me up this morning," and he agreed. We started getting more in-depth about God and life. I gave him some of my testimony and how God had changed my life. He started telling me that he went to the doctor, and they told him he was very ill and sick. They said he had cancer. He was so scared because his father and brother died from cancer, so he was afraid to die. They wanted to do more tests on him to see if it had spread to his bones. He said he was praying that God would send him an angel. We kept talking, and I was telling him about God's promises; that we go through different battles in life, but God always wins the war; how he lets us go through things to strengthen our faith and teach us different lessons. Being obedient is a lesson on how to be humble. God wants great faith and humility.

He was telling me his end-of-the-month check was for $696 a month, and after he paid his rent, he had to hustle up his light bill money. He talked about how he and his wife were always arguing, and she would just lie in bed with the pillow over her head. I told him, "That's how the devil works. He attacks the things you love the most, especially family. Remember God's promise: if two or more come together in his name, he shall bring it to pass. Keep fighting the battles because God will win the war. Have faith in God for the victory." He then said how he would like for his wife to come, so I gave him fifty dollars. I asked when he would be back up there, and he told me Thursday, if his ride got him there. He pointed to the parking lot, and it was a bike chained on a pole. I said, "I will see you again." I prayed with him and told him to be strong and to keep faith in God. I saw him about six months later at a store, and he remembered me and told others with him, "That's the man I was telling you about." I asked him how he was doing, and he told me all good news and all the things that happened in his life since I saw him last. I looked at him and said, "Prayer works. It's up to you."

## Testimony

I went out to feed fifty people today. After I finished, I hung around to talk and pray over the ones who wanted prayer and help some of those who needed money. This one guy listened and talked to me for a while. I blessed him with a small blessing, and he said, "Sir, I have a blessing for you." He started to sing "I Wish I Could Fly" by R. Kelly. He laid it out. This man could sing. Everyone started to come over and listen to him sing and cheer him on. I was looking into his face, and all I could see were bright lights. His eyes started to water, and you could tell he was singing this from his heart. Everyone there was just amazed at his talent and voice. After he finished, he walked over to me and said, "That's my gift to you." I gave him a hug, and I prayed over the group, leaving them with nothing but joy in my heart. I looked up at the sky and said, "God, this is why I do what I do."

## Testimony

Today I went out to feed fifty people at the Salvation Army shelter, where I go every week for the last fifteen years. I wanted to signal one person out of the hundreds who were out there. I had two old watches my son left behind. I put them in two separate bags and said, "Whoever comes to me and asks if I lost a watch while I am making the lunches, I will reward them every week." I was passing out the lunches and water when I got close to the end. Some older man said, "Did you lose a watch while you were preparing the lunches?" I just started smiling and told him the story about why I did that. We talked for a while, and I found out he was sixty years old, lived in Cincinnati for ten years, my hometown. He told me about how he lost his mother and three brothers and sister in three years, and he had back and nerve problems. That was how he lost everything. I gave him ten dollars and two new T-shirts. That's all I had with me. He was very happy for that and really appreciated the stuff I gave him. He had a girlfriend with him, and she was very sick. The day before, they had rushed her to the hospital, and they kept her. He was pretty sad about everything, especially after losing all his family members. I prayed with him, and after, I told him to put it in God's hands because he is the only one who can say when it's over. I saw him there a couple more weeks, and I was told he went back to Ohio.

*Testimony*

I woke up this morning feeling good. Somehow I knew it was going to be a great morning. I decided to hit the track at Webb Middle School and walk for a while and talk to God. I started walking. When I got to my second lap, I saw something in the dirt, and it was a teenage girl just lying there, not moving. It looked like she was dead. I started yelling out for help, and this Spanish guy was running on the track, and he told me she had been lying there since 8:00 a.m. It was about ten-thirty. I yelled at her, and she lifted her head and put it back down. It seemed like she just didn't care. She was lying in dirt, pale, face-first. The Spanish guy's wife went over to talk to her and gave her a bottle of water. We all walked to the parking lot to talk. I guess the teenager was not making sense.

The guy went into a building, and about ten minutes later, the police came and put her into the back of the police car. The officer who was on the radio told the other one she was a run-away, and she had been missing for a long time. At that time, tears started running down my face because she looked like my daughter, Alexis, and I knew she had a family who were look-ing for her for a long time. *Thanks, God, for sending me to walk today, and please keep using me to help others. Amen.*

*Testimony*

Our lives are measured on the footprints we leave behind. After church today, I went back to the park to feed like I do every week. I talked to one homeless gentleman who was so polite and respectful. We had an enjoyable conversation about life and God. He was a Vietnam vet. We talked about the war and some of the things he saw, the conditions and things he was surrounded with. One thing I noticed, he was in high spirits. You could tell that it was something he was proud of, fighting for his country. I could see that spark in his eyes, but at the same time, I could tell the damage it had done to him physically and mentally. He was suffering from a mental disfunction. He said the most thing he was proud of was his mother teaching him to always keep his head up, and he did that. He was about sixty years old. I thought that was powerful, for all that he had been through to remember that and to honor his mother. You see, sometimes when you're at the bottom, all you have is God and memories.

*Testimony*

My family left out about nine o'clock Christmas Day to go feed and give out our gifts to the homeless like we did every week, but on holidays, we would do some special things. We arrived downtown about nine-thirty. There were about one hundred people who were waiting on things. One great moment about the holidays was, a lot of givers come out to serve. After I got everyone in line, I had this one guy get out of the line and say, "You always are here helping us, and today I want to pray for you." Everyone started yelling yes and prayed over me. Afterward, we did our feeding and gave our gifts. On my way home, it hit me. Here was someone at the bottom of their life, and they were praying over me. This was, by far, the biggest gift I had received. A lot of times, we do things we think go unnoticed, but God never forgets, and we can never outgive God.

*Testimony*

In January, I had my brother-in-law come down to visit from my hometown of Cincinnati, Ohio. We could all celebrate our birthdays in the month of January. When they arrived, my wife and I were on a twenty-one-day fast, so we all talked about it, and I was telling them no birthday cake this year and all the other things we were sacrificing. I knew he wasn't a God-fearing man and didn't believe in God. Every time I got a chance, I told him about the goodness and grace of God. How God has changed my life and healed me from all the things I have been through. Back in the day, these guys wouldn't be holding a conversation with me because they were afraid of me. But the glory of Jesus Christ, my Lord and Savior, can change anything and everything.

The next day was Sunday, and my brother-in-law and sister went to church with us. My sister still goes to church every Sunday. She serves in the Catholic Church, and that's how our mother raised us. I left that religion and became nondenominational That is where I serve today. We got to church, and the choir started singing, and you could feel the presence of the Lord. I looked over and saw tears running down his face. I passed him a tissue, and when the pastor started preaching, I hollered out, "Preach, preach!" and he did just that. What a powerful service it was.

When we got home, he started asking questions. I kept answering them and telling him how God has been there for him. I told them there was a special guest coming from Puerto Rico on Wednesday, and they both wanted to go with us. I said that would be great. We were all sitting around talking, and he said, "I keep telling my wife that I had to get down here and see you. Even if I had to come by myself. I just knew I had to come." Something hit me. My Holy Spirit started preaching to him lightly every day. I told him about being a good husband, good father, good person; being faithful, obedient, humble; and reading the Bible every day. I said, "If you are smartest one in your group, you are in trouble," and we both started laughing. I told him the keys were there while they were here and go out and see Tampa and enjoy.

Wednesday came, and everyone was ready for church that day. We sat talking about life in general and the blessing and struggles that life brings you. We arrived at church around 7:00 p.m. The praise and worship was the best of the best. When the main speaker started, he was outstanding. Tears were rolling down everyone's face. There wasn't a dry eye in the church. I gave my brother-in-law some more tissue.

They started collecting tithes and offerings. I knew my sister tithes every week, but I knew this was his first time. That service was one of the top three I had witnessed there, and it really moved me. We got home and continued to talk about it. The next day was Thursday. We sat down in the family room and talked about the service again and about God. I could see an unusual look in my brother-in-law's face. It was a glow, like he had seen a ghost. He was asking a lot of questions about God and blessings. I asked him, had he given his life to God? and he said no. I asked him, would he like to give his life over to God and start over fresh? He said yes.

He gave his life to God that Thursday morning in my family room. I led him to prayer and told him when he got back home, find a good church he would like and get baptized. Slowly walk the walk. Try to live close to the Bible as possible. I also told him no one is perfect but God. He will make mistakes, repent, and get on those knees and ask God for forgiveness. I told him, "You must go through Jesus to get to his Father God and heaven." The next day was Friday, and I took them to the airport. They flew back to Cincinnati.

Every day I was looking to see what God was going to do for me through this fast. I was lying in bed daydreaming, and my Holy Spirit started talking to me. He told me about the gift. I helped lead someone to God. It's not about us all the time. God will use us to get to someone else. I talked to my sister a couple of days ago, and she said she could see him starting to change some. I told her it was a process. If a bird and fish fell in love, where would they live? Only God could make that happen.

# WHOSE EYES ARE YOU SEEING THROUGH

# CHAPTER 8

## Motivational Quotes

A winner is just a dreamer who never gave up
—Nelson Mendela

Sit in a special room or place you like that makes you happy or reminds you of something special and just dream. I've learned to dream for relaxation and peace.

You must take time with your children. Their peers have at least seven to eight hours a day while parents only have about three to four hours a day with them. Talk to your children at dinner or after school to find out what they are doing or thinking. Sometimes as parents, we think too much about bills, us and everything else, when we should be talking to our kids. Dig in their lives, make them talk to you. Parents, we must make them talk. Either we talk now, or we will cry later. Now is the time to find out what's going with them with school, peer pressure, drugs, or whatever it is. Let's catch it early.

*The question is not who is going to let
me . . . it's who is going to stop me.*

—Ayn Rand

*When everything seems to be going against you, remember
that the airplane takes off against the wind not with it.*

—Henry Ford

*Change your thoughts and you will change the world.*

—Norman Vincent Peale

*Either write something worth reading or
do something worth writing.*

—Benjamin Franklin

*Champions aren't made in gyms. Champions are made
from something they have deep inside them: a desire, a
dream, a vision. They have to have last minute stamina.
They have to be a little faster, they have to have the skill
and the will. But the will must be stronger than the skill.*

—Muhammad Ali

*Do not go through life wearing two catcher's mitt because
you need one hand free to throw something back.*

—Maya Angelou

*Men who have achieved great things have been dreamers.*
—Orison Swett Mardsen

*A man's dreams are an index to his greatness.*
—Zadok Rabinwitz

*Life is like riding a bicycle. You don't fall
off unless you stop pedaling.*
—Claude Pepper

*Life without love is like a tree without blossom and fruit.*
—Khail Gibran

*Your only obligation in any lifetime is to be true to yourself.*
—Richard Bach

*Let each day be your masterpiece.*
—John Wooden

*Our greatest glory is not in never failing
but in rising every time we fail.*
—Ralph Waldo

*If you don't know where you are going,*
*any road will get your there.*

—Lewis Carol

*Be wiser than other people if you can, but do not tell them so.*

—Dale Carnegie

*The journey of a thousand miles starts with a single step.*

—Lao Tru

*Success seems to be largely a matter of*
*hanging on after others have let go.*

—William Feather

*All great achievements require time.*

—Maya Angelou

*Remember, no one can make you feel*
*inferior without your consent.*

—Eleanor Roosevelt

*Don't compromise yourself. You are all you've got.*

—Janis Joplin

*The smallest good deed is greater than the grandest intention.*
—John Burroughs

*Patience is bitter, but fruit is sweet.*
—John Jacques Rousseau

*Nothing in life is to be feared; it is only to be understood.*
—Marie Curie

*About the only thing that comes without effort is old age.*
—Gloria Atzer

*Purpose is what gives life a meaning.*
—Charles Henry Parkhurst

*A wise man will make more opportunities than he finds.*
—Sir Francis Baron

*Choice, not chance, determines destiny*
—Regina Brett

*Winning isn't everything; it's the only thing.*
—Vince Lombardi

*The harder you work, the luckier you get.*
—Ben Franklin

*There is always room at the top.*
—Ganna Walsko Lotusland

*Life is my college.*
—Louisa May Alcott

*To succeed, we must first believe that we can.*
—Michael Korda

*Nothing is impossible to a willing heart. You
cannot do wrong without suffering wrong.*
—John Heyward

*If there is a way to do, better find it.*
—Thomas Jefferson

*Never, never, never quit.*
—Winston Churchill

*Good is not good where better is expected.*

—Vin Scully

*Ingenuity plus courage plus work equals miracles.*

—Bob Ricardo

*Act as though it were impossible to fail.*

—Dorathea Brande

*Paralyze resistance with persistence.*

—Woody Hayes

*Desire creates the power.*

—Raymond Holliwell

*There is no right way to do the wrong thing.*

—Harold S. Kushner

*A will finds a way.*

—Orison Swett Mardsen

*In the middle of difficulty lies opportunity.*

—Albert Einstein

*A wise man will make more opportunity than he finds.*
—Francis Barone

*God is in control. He is doing a work in you.*
*He is guiding and directing you.*

*If you are currently in a storm, or if you're facing*
*some severe difficulties, God is speaking to your heart*
*these words—Rise above it. Quit fighting. Quit*
*trying to change things that only I can change.*

*God is going to fight your battles for you; that is what it says in the*
*book of Exodus, chapter 14. If you will remain at rest and hold*
*your peace, then the battle is not yours, but the battle is the Lord's.*

*Weeping may endure for a night, but joy cometh in the*
*morning. As much as you desire to become a better you, it is*
*important to understand that not everything God does is about*
*you. Sometimes God asks you to suffer for somebody else.*

*For the resolute and determined, there is time and opportunity.*
—Ralph Waldo Emerson

*All our dreams come true if we have the courage to pursue them.*
—Walter E. Disney

*The greatest mistake a man can make*
*is to be afraid of making one.*
—Albert Hubbard

*The successful man will profit from his mistakes*
*and try again in a different way.*
—Dale Carnegie

*Excellence is to do a common thing in an uncommon way.*
—Booker T. Washington

*The most important thing about goals is having one.*
—Geoffrey F. Albert

*Prefer a loss to a dishonest gain. The one brings*
*pain in the moment the other for all time.*
—Chilon

*Honest is the first chapter of the book of wisdom.*
—Thomas Jefferson

*You can be in the storm but cannot let the storm get in you.*
—Joel Osteen

*Anytime you obey God, a blessing will follow.*
—Joel Osteen

*Nothing is impossible to a willing heart.*

*Ask God to give you strength to endure. Remember
the good things God does or has done.*

*We must obey God today so he can fix our tomorrow.*

*Ask God to me who I am so I may be myself.*

*Sometimes you don't where you there is.
You just know you are not there.*
—Leigh Ashton

*If you can see the invisible, you can do the impossible.*
—Joel Osteen

*I will, I can, I must.*
—Eric Thomas

# WHOSE EYES ARE YOU SEEING THROUGH

# CHAPTER 9

## *Faith*

I was asked to write this book from a lot of people I've talked to or helped along the way. I told them my life story, of all the trials and tribulations I have been through and all the blessings I had received. I was never supposed to make it out of the hood. Most of us don't. If you ask Vegas, the odds are fifty to one. By the age of thirty, I would have been in prison or dead. I've seen that happen so many times. A lot of my friends are dead, in jail, or still doing the same things. The best happened to me is I never should stop dreaming about things outside the hood, going places, or living around the world. I wasn't afraid of anything except of God. All the things I've been through, I knew it had to be something special God had for me. I just learned to trust him and have faith. Through my journey, it's been some great stops and some not so pleasant. I always kept in mind I was here or doing this for a reason. God took me through everything he used me for. Now I look back and smile when I see the finished product of what I was doing and remembered that God would not send you to do something unless he had you prepared for the task. Remember, he will not put more on you than you can bear. To that one person who feels that they are alone, you're not. There is a God who loves you. He will teach you and heal and guide you. He is bigger than any name, situation, or problem. All you need to have is faith and love. You see, he took a nasty person like me, broke me down, and rebuilt me in his likeness. God taught me how to love and have kindness to help others.

My foundation feeds over five thousand people alone. I would have never thought about this growing up in my hood. The streets taught me to be first and not to worry about anyone else. But glory to Jesus Christ, my Lord and Savior, because he will rebuild you and take away all those bad teaching and habits. I am not perfect, and I am different. I'm not the person I used to be. It's so funny because when I first got saved twenty-five years ago. I thought everything would go fast, and I would learn everything overnight and be this perfect person. I learned that no one is perfect but God. He has perfect timing and will do things on his time, not ours. You know how you feel when you want something so bad, and it doesn't happen? Stop and ask yourself, is this God's will? Remember, he promised he wouldn't put on you more than you can bear. I always say, "God, make me rich, do this or that." Then I stopped because I know that's my flesh talking, not my heart. I've learned to be patient, humble, and obedient because when God wants me to have something, nothing can stop him giving me whatever his heart desires.

Every day, I just try to be a better person in a godly way by helping more people, trying to inspire, spreading the gospel, read and telling life story.

Everyone who knows me back home will tell you about me. I was a mess. God had a lot of cleaning up to do. If he can clean me up and fix the broken pieces on me, he can fix anything or person. Praise the Lord. Come out of those dark corners. Come out of those neighborhoods, trailer parks, or whatever you're watching out of. Come out watching people getting shot, going to jail, seeing drugs being sold, watching your kids dropping out of school with no dreams. Come out, come out, wherever you are.

I learned the poorest person in the world is not a person without money but a person without dreams. Don't be afraid to dream. Think big, think worldwide. I always dream big. I would go and sit in a new car and look at houses that cost a lot, or a nice hotel that costs a lot of money that I couldn't afford. One of my biggest dreams is feeding one million people. On some Saturdays, I go out and do a YouTube segment called "Walking the Street with Amos." I go out to the areas where my foundation feeds people, and I sit down and talk to everyone about life, and I ask them, if they could change the world, what would they change? You would be surprised by some of the intelligent ideas people come up with. I do this to bring people to dreaming and thinking. I always say, if you're the smartest person in your group, you are in trouble. Find someone whom you look up to like a pastor, an older relative, or just pick up a book and read. I read the Bible over and over, and every time I read it, I find out something I didn't understand before. That's what made me guide my life around scriptures and try to live accordingly to the lessons. It took me a while to understand that God knows that we are not perfect in any way, shape, or form.

But he expects us to know the difference between right and wrong and act accordingly.

It's funny because most people think that just because they go to church on Sunday, they are a good Christian; and right when church is over, they go back to their weekly habits again. They don't practice what they read or preach about. I tell people that if I sat in my garage, would that make me a car? That really helped me out trying to do the right thing. Even when it came to tithing my 10 percent. I always make that happen if it's my last or a late bill or an expense that came up. I would make sure my tithes were first. Another thing I learned is, you can't outgive God. There would be times I would give my last to help someone else and not worry. I have faith that God will always bless me no matter what the circumstances are. He has always come through.

This chapter is dedicated to someone like me, who was lost, didn't trust anyone, and lived in a dark hole, thinking no one loves me or cared about me. Everything was a fight, and I had to win at all cost, no matter what. I am here to tell you about a man names Jesus, our Lord and Savior. He will love you, care for you, mend your broken heart, heal you, bless you, and most of all save you. All you have to do is accept him as your Lord and Savior and have faith in him. Remember, God will do things in his time line not ours. So be patient and humble.

# WHOSE EYES ARE YOU SEEING THROUGH

# CHAPTER 10

## Blessings and Favor

It took a lot for me to leave Cincinnati, Ohio, as I was saying in chapter 1. A lot of things were going on, and as I look back at the time, now I understand God had a lot of favor and blessings over my life because of my vision of wanting to get away or had to get away. It reminded me of God telling Moses about leaving and how he had to leave alone, not taking anyone with him, or it would be trouble—the same thing my mother told me when I had to leave home. I saw my path out, even when no one else was seeing me get away. It wasn't easy at time. Everyone was going to jail and getting killed. Even some were overdosing on drugs and dying. It was a big mess. I know it was favor when my Holy Spirit stopped me from going from back to Steve's house that same day he got caught with that robbery and murder charge. Now I have the opportunity to look back at all the things God has done for me and my family.

I remember here in Tampa I got a letter from a big-time attorney from Miami, telling me his client was suing me and eighty-nine other businesses in Tampa for handicap violations.

I met with my attorney to try to stop this. We talked about it, and he said, "Let me check it out and get back to you." I told him okay. I just kept thinking I could not afford a lawsuit; that would destroy everything I had worked for. My attorney got back with me in a couple of days and said, "This is a big-time law firm in Miami, and what they are doing is going to every city in the state of Florida, suing every business that does not have a handicap bathroom. They said their client was unable to use your facility, although the client had never been to your establishment." They sent a person to your establishment and took pictures. I was renting the space out as a restaurant, and it was up to the business owners to make sure he was in code, but they sued me, the property owner.

My attorney said everyone was paying them out to stop from going to court, and they were charging anywhere from five to ten thousand dollars to each business, depending on the size. My jaw dropped when he told me that. I told my attorney that I was going to call them and see if they would drop it, and he said they were getting settlements from big business owners who were paying them off. I told him, "Let me just call and talk to them and try." The next morning, I got their number and called them. One of the smaller attorneys from their firm got on the phone, and I told him my name, and I was the property owner, not the business owner. I also told him that I was a 100 percent disabled veteran, and I was selling the property. I asked him, could he take my name off that lawsuit because he was suing the business owner also? And he said, "No, when you sell the property, I will draw up the paperwork saying you will give up five thousand dollars." I said again, "Sir, I am a 100 percent disabled vet like your client." He kept saying, "Five thousand dollars, or we are going to court." Something inside me was saying, *Tell him we will see him in court.* So I did.

Later that day, I told my attorney what had happened and how I said, "I will see you in court." My attorney said we should have just paid them the money because in court, we would have to pay what they were asking for and attorney's fees, all together about fifty to one hundred thousand dollars. All the other businesses paid them off, and we were the only ones going to court. I don't think my attorney was afraid of going to court; I think he was afraid for me paying all that money for the loss. He knew how I fed the homeless and gave things to people who were in need and how this had been my life, helping others and spreading the word. I just told him to let me know when the court date came in, and he looked at me strangely and said okay. I saw a glow in his face; it was all lit up.

I had started getting sick, and when the court date came up, he called me that night before and said, "We have to be there at nine-thirty." I told him he had to go alone, and I had paperwork from the doctor saying I was on bed rest for two weeks more. He said, "Okay, and if the judge needs a copy, you will have to fax it to me." I then told him not to worry because Jesus was with him, and he said, "I will call you after court." Around eleven o'clock, he called me and said, "You're not going to believe this." I could hear the joy in his voice. He said, "You won, you won!" Out of eighty something businesses, you were the only one that beat them. The judge gave you the right to get all your attorney fees back up to fifty thousand dollars. We could charge them fifty thousand, and they would have to pay it. He couldn't believe we won the case. I told my wife what happened, and she was very happy also. Then I said to her, "Remember when we bought that building? When it was empty, I prayed in that building, walking all through it, asking God to be our partners in business." And she said, "Yes, I remember." Two days later, that same attorney from that law firm in Miami called me, and he was a different person. I told him that I was not going to be like his law firm and try to take advantage of people trying to make it. I said, "If I hear of anyone complaining about you guys again, I am coming after you with my judgement that I won in court." He said, "Yes, sir," and I never heard from them again. I told my attorney that I was not going to give him any of that money because that would make me like them: *greedy*. When you put God in business with you, you have to remember who you are in partners with, and to raise your standards because he will not lower his.

We decided to downsize from our five-bedroom to something a little smaller. My daughter, Alexis, wanted to go to a high school out of our district, so we were looking at houses in this one particular area, near the school she liked. I said, "I will pray over the move." We started looking more and more in that area, and everything we saw we didn't feel a connection. We decided to go one day without our agent. We were driving through the neighborhood, and I told my wife, "Stop the car. This house, back up the car." There was about four guys out doing the grass and trimming the bushes. She looked at me with that look and said, "This house is not for sale." There were no signs, fliers, or nothing to show it was for sale. My Holy Spirit said, *This is the house where you will be doing Bible study and bringing people to God*. I got out of the car and walked up to this one guy who was on his cellphone and asked if this house was for sale. He looked at me real strange, but I could see the light all over his face.

He then said, "Yes, sir, I'm talking to the agent now." I got her information and told her my agent would call her. I got back into my car, and my wife said, "How did you know that house was for sale?" I smiled and said, "My Holy Spirit said I would be having Bible study there and bringing people to the Lord," and she just smiled.

I talked to my agent to set up an appointment so we could see the inside. He also said, "How did you know it was for sale? I talked to the agent, and they haven't put it on the market yet, and they haven't done anything other than get it ready." I told him what I told my wife. That Monday, we went to see the house, and it was beautiful. My Holy Spirit was telling me what things were going to happen in this house. How I was going to bring family and others to this house for peace and prayer. We took care of all the paperwork, and the next month, we moved in. That was five years ago. My wife and I have brought family and friends here and got them back on the right track, prayed over them, and taught them to always love God first. This same house is where an atheist gave his life to God, and I led him in prayer.

My wife and I decided to refinance our commercial property. We went to this credit union and inquired about it, and they said their real estate guy would call us later that day. He called, and we started talking about what I was trying to do. My wife explained everything to him and did the application online, and he said, "I will check everything out and get back with you. I said thanks, and we didn't talk for a couple of days. We received a call from him, and he wanted to meet us. We met with him and my wife, and I sat down to talk, and we found out he had worked for the bank that we were trying to leave. He said, "I remember this property. This property here we were trying to take back in

2008. That was when the market dropped, and everyone was losing their houses and businesses. The bank had me in court every day, taking two or more properties a day." He kept saying how the bank was trying to take my building. I remember we were behind on the mortgage about three months. I did the paperwork to pay the interest-only loan until we could catch up on the loan. I remember them telling me that I was still going to be foreclosed on. I just kept praying like I did when we bought it when it was empty, and I prayed and asked God to be a partner in business with us. A lot of people were losing everything.

In 2007, 2008, and 2009, it was unbelievable how the market and the economy had fallen. My guy from the credit union kept telling us they were trying to take that property away. After meeting him, I could tell it was something personal. He kept telling my wife and I that I was a closer, and he kept repeating it. He said, "Give me all your financial statements and other paperwork, and I will look at everything and see if the loan would go through." He said I had to get the restaurant lease out because the other two spaces were already on a three-year contract, and that was good. But I knew he was looking for a reason to turn this loan down. He was upset he didn't foreclose on this property when he was with the other company. He asked me and my wife not to mention him to the old company he had worked for, the ones that we were trying to get away from. It's funny how things work out with God.

Later that day, we leased the restaurant out on a three-year lease. I forwarded him the paperwork, so this would not hold up the process. I called him up every day, and he would tell me that he was waiting on the paperwork. On the eighth day, he finally called me back and said that the loan was disapproved because I lied on the application. I told him I already had the restaurant rented out. He said I lied and never told him that and he saw it was empty. He said he saw it was empty and asked when it would be rented out, and I told him I had three applications and were looking at them to choose the right tenant to put in there. He said, regardless, they already turned us down. I knew this guy just wanted revenge. I asked my wife to find out who was the top in charge. She found out who he was. He was in a different city, and I said, "Let's go there to see him without an appointment or telephone call." I just showed up. I was listening to my Holy Spirit.

My wife and I went there, and when we arrived, no one could get past the security guard at the desk. You couldn't get on the elevator to get to the third floor. We asked the guard, could he ask the head guy if we could talk to him? And he did. The head guy said he was leaving out, headed to a meeting somewhere else. Thirty seconds later, the elevator came down to the first floor, he got out, and walked over to my wife and me, and said, "Are you Amos Allen?" I said, "Yes sir." He said, "I'm sorry that I am leaving, but my next person in charge will help you out." He told the security to give us a badge we needed to get to his office, and he would call and have the lady waiting on us. We told him thanks, and he shook our hands and left. There was something special about that meeting. When we got upstairs, three ladies were waiting on us, and all of them were nice and professional. We straightened out all the paperwork, got everything done we needed to do, and the loan was approved with the guy who was trying to stop it. Little did he know that when he kept calling me the closer, it was the right terminology but the wrong person. God is the closer.

# WHOSE EYES ARE YOU SEEING THROUGH

# CHAPTER 11

## *It's Never Over*

I had begun to get very sick, and I made a doctor's appointment at the VA hospital. I arrived at the hospital and talked to my doctor about what was going on with me. He said we are going to do some labs and other tests so we can determine what was going on. We finished everything, and they scheduled me to come back to see a specialist in two weeks. Finally, after the two weeks had passed, I got to that doctor at 9:45 a.m., still not feeling so well. The doctor took me back to his office and told me I had lost a lot of blood and started asking me a lot of questions. Had I been in an accident, or had I been bleeding anywhere? I said no. What was wrong? He said, "I think you might be anemic. We're going to do some blood test and bring you back in this afternoon."

I got a call that afternoon, and they said they were making me another doctor's appointment, and they would be notified by that office. The next week, I received a card in the mail for an appointment with the hematology clinic for that following week. I was just telling my family I would find out that problem, and they could fix it. We would be done with that. My whole body was hurting, and I was getting sick to my stomach, and my bones were hurting. I kept saying it must not be anything serious because my doctor did not call me back in. He just referred me to another clinic in the hospital.

Time went by, and finally the morning arrived for my appointment. I was so excited they found the problem, and we would find out the results. I was sitting in the waiting area, and my name was called to go the nurses' station. I was just smiling and singing to myself. The doctor said, "Sit down there," and he was putting information into his computer. He said, "I am assigning you to your oncology team," and he looked at me and said, "How long have you had it?" I said, "Had what?" And he said, "Cancer." I said, "What!" real loud. He said, "Didn't your doctor tell you that you have cancer? Multiple myeloma." He said that it was a bone cancer, and it was terminal. Inside, my head and body wanted to explode. This was my first time hearing this. I just sat there and held everything back—tears, rage, emotions—and it was very difficult. He saw the rage on my face.

The other nurse came and took me to be weighed in and to take my vital signs. I was still holding all this emotional and anger inside me and trying to smile. She finished all her work, and she told me to go back into the waiting room. I started people-watching. I have heard a lot about cancer and lost my oldest sister Mary to cancer. I was seeing how most of the people there were so sick, and the smell hit me. It smelled like sickness. The whole time I was sitting there, I was still holding everything inside me. Finally, the nurse practitioner called me in, and we started talking about my lab results, and he was telling me about the cancer that I had. There was no cure, and most people lived up to five years with this type. He was setting me up with the oncology doctor so we could start some treatment. He also said how sorry he was for the way I found out. He said the right treatment could help me stay alive a little longer but that it was terminal; there is no cure. He asked me if there were any more questions, and I said no. I just wanted to get out of there. He said he was bringing me back in about two weeks to meet my doctor and start talking treatment. I left still speaking and smiling to people, saying, "Have a great day" and "God bless you."

I walked out that hospital and got into my car. I looked at the picture of my wife and daughter and just lost it. Tears just started falling down my face, and I was just so angry. I was so mad at God and everyone. I kept saying, "God, I do everything you tell me. I quit smoking, drinking, partying. I feed about twenty-five thousand people, clothe them, give them money, kind words, tell people how great you are and all you do for people. You let me get cancer." I was so angry and afraid about what I was going to tell my wife and daughter. When I got home, I told my wife the results, and we both started crying together. I wasn't afraid for me; it was about my wife and daughter living alone. My wife told my daughter when she got home. My daughter came to my bedroom and gave me a big hug and said, "Daddy, we are with you no matter what. We are with you." That gave me strength, knowing I didn't have to worry about them.

When I finally got back to my doctor, the oncologist started telling me how long she had been doing cancer work and where she had been working, all the different VA hospitals. We started talking about my condition, and she told me about all the tests that they had done on me. She told me I was a good candidate for a stem cell transplant, and the VA would pay for it if I qualified for it. She told me there was a battery of tests I would go through. I would even have to see a phycologist. There are only two places in the United States where VA does these types of transplants: one in Texas and one in Tennessee. I would be there for three to four months depending on the success or outcome of the transplant. One good thing I had going for me was, I would be using my own stem cells. This was a lot to digest in one day. The hardest part about this was my wife would have to go with me. She is my health-care provider. She would have to leave her job and not work for three to four months.

It's not a hard decision because my life doesn't have a price tag on it. I think I am worth all the money in the world. My faith hasn't left me. There are times when the enemy will try to play games with us like a battlefield of the mind, but I stay focused and started talking about my treatment. We waited for about six weeks, and my numbers were getting higher. My treatment consisted of taking Revlimid, which is a strong cancer medication taken once in the morning. She also put me on steroids once a week, taking ten pills every Saturday. Both meds, I had to take the maximum, and that combination together was very tough. I started this treatment at the end of 2015. During this time, my doctor put me in for all the evaluations and appointments. My wife and I started talking about picking up another insurance to stay in Tampa. We could use Moffitt Cancer Hospital. My numbers were going down after I started taking the medication. Everything was looking good.

One day I was lying in bed talking to God and saying, "You promised you would protect me and let nothing harm me. This is your promise." My Holy Spirit started talking back to me, saying, *I never promised that you wouldn't go through anything. Where is your faith, and where is your strength? What about your promise you made to me? That if I saved you twenty years ago, you would feed the homeless for the rest of your life? Get up out of that bed and keep your promise. Stop having a pity party for yourself.* That Saturday morning, I was back out there feeding the homeless.

I remember hearing that same voice when I was in the hospital with a bullet in my head that caused another bleed in 2001. I just didn't see the faces. I go out every third Saturday to feed, clothe, and give money to the homeless. I stuck to my word, and God did the same. Money came in for the new insurance, and all my tests were coming back good.

I was talking to a doctor at one of my appointments, and she was looking at her computer, and she stopped and looked at me. She said, "Mr. Allen, are you a religious man?" I said, "Yes," and she said, "I can tell." I knew God was all over me, guiding me and protecting me. The next couple of weeks taking all those meds was very rough for me. I had some challenging times, but I kept focusing on day-to-day prayer and just asking God to give me another day. A lot of people don't understand cancer, and it's very hard to explain because you have to go through so much, and it's very hard to deal with alone. You have to have a support system, and even better if you have God.

On my next visit, I told my VA doctor that I had an appointment at Moffit Cancer Center. My wife and I decided I would have the stem cell transplant there. We had to go through another round of the same to qualify for the transplant. My visit at Moffit was different. I was seeing people who were sick like me with all kinds of cancer. All the things I heard about people's hair was falling out, losing weight, couldn't walk. There were others like me who were holding on to God's word. I knew this a tough fight, and I had to win with me first before I could have a support team. Only I knew what I was going through. It's up to me every day, minute, second to choose to go on or give up, and a lot of people give up. I always say if I give up, who could tell my story like me? I see through these eyes.

I remember one day I was feeding the homeless, and one of the guys said, "Sir, I'd like you to meet someone," and he introduced me to this old guy named James. We started talking, and he told me he just got out of prison and gave his life to the Lord when he first went in about twenty years ago. He also told me he was diagnosed with AIDS a year after he was put in jail. He also said he was innocent from the crime. Check this out, twenty years in jail and never been treated for AIDS, ever had any medicine at all. I kept talking to him, and I could see the glow all over his face. His friend told me he had never talked to anyone like he did with me. These are some of the things I see with my eyes while I'm fighting this monster (cancer).

What do you see out of your eyes, because you have to recognize it to fight it? A lot of sick people don't see their self healthy or whole; they just take medicine and go into a depression and give up. Who's telling your story? In some of my weak days, I would sit back and reminisce about going to feed and clothe the homeless. When I got in the area, they would see my black truck, and everyone would come running, saying "The man with the black truck is here." I had this guy ask me why they called me the man with the black truck, and I said, "I never told them my name," and he asked why. I told him all the praise go to Jesus Christ, my Lord and Savior. If I told them my name, they would be calling me by my name, and I always told them Jesus was sending me.

I remember one day I was there passing out money. I went to the bank and got two hundred dollars in fives. I had about fifty people in line, and I thought, *I will keep giving until I run out of money.* Something happened, and I gave everyone I had in line five dollars. I had ten dollars left in my truck, and I cried and pointed up to heaven, and I told God thanks because I witnessed a miracle. We all have something to go back to when we are down or sick, no matter what we are going through. What you see in your eyes will tell your story. It's up to you. These are some of the things that keep me inspired and want to live and not give up. Who will tell your story?

God never promised we will not go through anything, so every day, I ask him to give me strength to endure what I'm going through.

Today is the day for my transplant. We got to Moffit Cancer Center at 5:00 a.m. They had to collect about fifty thousand stem cells, and they said, "Don't be alarmed because sometimes people have to come for two days to get this done." But I kept thinking about me. God has something special for me. The doctor said I wouldn't be finished until about 3:00 or 4:00. I was done at eleven 11:45 a.m., and they collected one million. The nurse called me an overachiever. I didn't have to come back the next day. On the third day, they gave me an overdose of chemo to kill all the bacteria in my body. I got home that night. It was bad, and I mean bad. All the medication I was on and the chemo just made me sick. I wouldn't wish this on my worst enemy. All my hair fell out; I had a bald head. I was sick every day from the chemo. The doctor was telling me and my wife that it was very important to make sure that I eat and drink, or they would have to put me in the hospital. Like I said, I can do all things through Jesus Christ, who strengthens me. I started eating and drinking like a champ. My doctor would look at our morning chart and just smile. He could not believe how I was getting through this with no complications. I was thinking Mark 1:40–42: "A man with leprosy came to him and begged him on his knees, if you are willing, you can make me clean. Jesus was indignant. He reached out his hand and touched the man. I am willing he said; be clean. Immediately, the leprosy left him, and he was cleansed."

I always think of that verse when I am sick or going through something that's hard to deal with. I think we should all have something that makes us smile or be happy—a Bible verse, a song, or whatever it is. We should have something to inspire us.

During my ninety-day checkup back at Moffit Cancer Center, my oncology doctor ran every test you could on me. We could find out if the stem cell transplant worked. I found out later that day everything was looking good. My red and white blood cells where growing back, and I noticed some of my hair was even growing back. This was good news everything was going in the right direction. The best news is that I am in remission. That is great for this type of cancer because it is terminal. My doctor was telling me *remission* means we slow everything down for a moment, but it could come right back. I will be on the same cancer medication, just not as much. She would be adding a bone medicine that I would be taking through an IV every ninety days. This medicine would strengthen my bones. The bone cancer would destroy my bones and make them break easily. It has strong side effects.

The first time I got it was hell. I was shaking like drugstore craps, fever, chills, stomach sickness, and was extremely weak. I had to wait for sixty days for it to be out of my system. It was just another task on my journey. People ask me all the time, "Are you worried or afraid?" And I tell them, "I don't worry about things I cannot control and do not see." I've been like this all my life. I'm a strong guy.

Today I was looking at some of the things I've done. I've taught martial arts all over the United States. I always said I was in business with God. My theory was, if I could get one person to believe in themselves, then there wasn't any limitation of what they could learn or do. Even today, when I'm talking about life, cancer, or any other diseases, remember it's up to you; it's how you handle things or start your morning or make adjustments throughout your day. We all have difficult things we will have to deal with on an everyday basis, but a lot of time, we forget who we are and the power we have over things. Wake up. We are not victims. Dig into your strength. God gave us strength to concur all things in his name. But we cannot straddle the line and one day be good guys and the next week be bad guys. God said, "Choose life or death." Some of us don't like to hear that because we like to interpret the Bible to fit our situation. That is not right. God knows we are not perfect. Therefore, he has grace over us and not the law. We know the difference between right and wrong. What helps me a lot before I do something that's hectic or I'm not sure about, I ask myself what Jesus would do. This brings me back to my level head of thinking and decision-making.

Every time God takes me through something, he uses me in that situation. My long dream is my family foundation to build a large building, bring the homeless in on a rotation program for thirty days, clean them up, give them medical attention, find programs and work for the ones who can work and guide them, and help them with local and city programs. I am writing this when I was feeding one of the homeless. He said to me, "Sir, you are always helping us and praying over us, and today, sir, I want us to pray over you." That was a great feeling, having someone who's out of everything praying over me. You might not see the material things on them, but you would see the best things they have and an unselfish heart. I was always said you reap what you sow. The foundation will continue to serve and help others. I've been invited to share my journey with others and spread the gospel all over, and I will be doing whatever God has for me.

I will not lie in bed and have a pity party for myself about this cancer or any other problems. I will fight to my last breath and help others who choose to fight also. Remember, it's up to you!

# FAITH

# WHOSE EYES ARE YOU SEEING THROUGH

## FEATURE STORY

# Family Launches Holiday Tradition Of Giving Back

BY IRIS B. HOLTON
Sentinel Staff Writer

The holidays are the perfect time for companies and other organizations to take the opportunity to help the less fortunate. But, we seldom hear of just one family single-handedly taking on this awesome responsibility.

However, this is exactly what Mr. and Mrs. Amos (Heather) Allen and their children, Anthony, 13, and Nichole, 4, are doing. The family has already begun their effort of helping twenty families have an enjoyable Thanksgiving Holiday.

Recently, Allen delivered turkeys with all the trimmings to Mrs. Mary Davis, and Ms. Lisa Rouse. He was acquainted with the Davis Family, but was referred to the Rouses.

This marks the second year that the Allen family has participated in such an act of kindness. Last year, Allen, who owns and operates Amos

Amos Allen, of Amos Bail Bondsman Company, presented a complete Thanksgiving dinner to Ms. Lisa Rouse in an effort to give back to the community.

Amos Allen, of Amos Bail Bondsman Company, presented a complete Thanksgiving dinner to Mrs. Mary Davis, who recently lost her son.

# Businessman's Family Gives To Young, Single Mothers

BY IRIS B. HOLTON
Sentinel Staff Writer

There is an old adage that suggests you should not judge another person until you "walk a mile in his shoes." And while most are familiar with the saying many have never found themselves in situations that prove devastating to others.

As the Thanksgiving holiday approached in 1996, Amos Allen found himself in a position where he could have used some help. He had injured his back and wasn't sure how he would provide for his family. He recalls "praying for a basket" that year.

But it was also at that time that he vowed to help others who find themselves in need during the Thanksgiving and Christmas holiday.

Amos Allen of Amos Bail Bonds is shown with Ms. Yolanda Binder and her family with the holiday gift box presented to them.

Amos is shown displaying the holiday feast presented to Ms. Natasha Cook and her family.

Single moms I help every chance I have.

Feeding the homeless. Our foundation has
fed about twenty-five thousand so far.

Feeding the homeless.

Passing the money cards.

Amos training in Korea

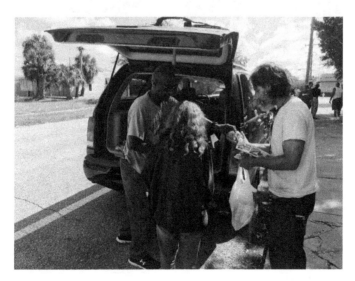

Feeding the homeless out the back of my car

School trophies ss

Anthony Allen, Superbowl champ, running back

Praying and feeding those without

# FINAL WORDS FROM THE AUTHOR

My final words are to tell you to keep looking out of your own eyes. No one can see your vision better than you. Follow God's voice and directions. Stay humble and obedient. No matter where you came from or how you look, God loves everyone. Keep your faith and dreams alive and always remember the poorest person in the world is not a person without money. It's a person without dreams. You can be whatever you want in life, but remember, you must put in the work. Everything you do or say in life is up to you. That's the whole story. Here now is my conclusion. Fear God and obey his commands, for this is everyone's duty (Ecclesiastes 12:13, NLV).

ABOUT THE AUTHOR

Amos Allen was born in raised in Cincinnati, Ohio, the only son of seven siblings. He was born in a low-poverty area in the housing projects of the Cincinnati area. He can remember being told that they would be there for the rest of their lives and would not amount to anything. He was also told he would not live to see twenty-one. He was shot five times and was involved in activities that were not good. There were no positive role models, no father, or male figure to install dreams, visions, or aspirations for kids in these types of areas. Amos Allen is now the president of the Amos Allen Family Foundation. He is also medically retired from the United States Army and holds a seventh-degree black belt in professional Tae Kwon Do. He is also a thirty-second Mason. He is one of the very few African Americans who taught martial arts in Korea. He has also taught martial arts all over the United States. He taught kids and adults martial arts and how to succeed and have a strong desire to accomplish the things they go after in life.

Amos has taught kids from the Juvenile Justice Center, Axe Program, and children's home. He also has five others in his school to become US Open World Champions. He has a strong desire to help kids and adults with some positive motivational speaking that is in his heart. This comes from where he used to be, to where he is now, to where he is going. He has taught and guided both of his young kids—Anthony Allen, at the age of five years—how to play football and martial arts. He won two US Open World Championships in fighting. He also holds two college titles at Louisville for the most yards in a single game: 275 yards rushing in a game. He also went on to be drafted in the NFL by the Baltimore Ravens, in which he helped take to the Superbowl and win.

Amos started teaching his daughter Alexis to play basketball at the age of five. She grew to competing with some of the best in the country. She is a known player in the AAU Basketball, and she helped take her high school team to the state championship game. She was scouted by some good college teams, who offered scholarships. She decided to stop playing to work more toward her degree. Amos taught his children that hard work pays the bills. It doesn't matter where you come from or how you look. The only thing that matters is, you must work hard for your dreams to come true and be humble, faithful, and obedient. The whole time, it was Jesus Christ, our Lord and Savior, who has kept me safe from the beginning of my journey and life.

CPSIA information can be obtained
at www.ICGtesting.com
Printed in the USA
FFHW02n0708171018
48836426-53038FF